I'm a New Dad!

3 minute prayers for new dads
...just add coffee & chocolate!

David Gatward

kevin mayhew

kevin
mayhew

First published in Great Britain in 2017 by Kevin Mayhew Ltd
Buxhall, Stowmarket, Suffolk IP14 3BW
Tel: +44 (0) 1449 737978 Fax: +44 (0) 1449 737834
E-mail: info@kevinmayhew.com

www.kevinmayhew.com

© Copyright 2017 David Gatward

The right of David Gatward to be identified as the author of this work has been asserted by him in accordance with the Copyright, Designs and Patents Act 1988.

All rights reserved. No part of this publication may be reproduced, stored in a retrieval system, or transmitted, in any form or by any means, electronic, mechanical, photocopying, recording, or otherwise, without the prior written permission of the publisher.

Scriptures quoted are from the Good News Bible © 1994 published by the Bible Societies/HarperCollins Publishers Ltd UK, Good News Bible© American Bible Society 1966, 1971, 1976, 1992. Used with permission.

9 8 7 6 5 4 3 2 1 0

ISBN 978 1 84867 917 7
Catalogue No. 1501555

Cover design by Rob Mortonson
© Image used under licence from Shutterstock Inc.
Edited by Helen Jones
Typeset by Angela Selfe

Printed and bound in Great Britain

For Elijah and Gabriel

Contents

Foreword	6
About the author	7
Introduction	8
The News	10
What IS That?	12
How Much?	14
Right, Here We Go …	16
He's Blue …	18
The Weight of Life	20
First Night	24
Chocolate	26
Work	28
Who We Are	30
Tag Team	32
Puke Face	34
Sex	36
Death	38

Night Drive	40
I'm No Good at This	44
Date Night	48
Baby Food	52
The Timetable	56
Reading	58
What About Me?	60
What If I'm Not a Good Dad?	64
Nappies	68
Natural Bond	70
Career Vs Dad	72
Separate Beds	76
Laugh	79
First Words	80
Just the Beginning …	82
An Amazing Mum	86

Foreword

Are they breathing? You run to your newborn's cot in panic. You move, trying to combine speed and stealth. Your heart racing and your mind screaming to God, 'Let them be ok.' Watching for the smallest rising and falling of a chest! Amazing really, because two hours earlier you were pleading with the heavens to give you an instant sleep secret that would work that night! As you stand there seeing air fill those little lungs, you get that feeling which is still new. A sense of being totally overwhelmed by love in a way never experienced.

That's fatherhood. All the clichés are true – it is a world-changing experience. The love, the joy and the realisation you are not in control. Working out what this means for you as a man and what it means for your relationship with your partner.

That's why this book is ridiculously helpful. David's prayers are refreshingly honest, real and life-giving. This book helps to give you a framework to cry out your joy, pain, doubt and unknowing to God.

Learn to be honest with God about how you are feeling as you embark on the most important job you'll ever do. It will help you feel better about yourself and when we feel better about who we are, we pass that joy to our children.

Enjoy being a dad – it is the most amazing and bonkers thing you'll ever do.

Richard Shorter, father of three, church minister and parenting coach.
www.non-perfectdad.co.uk

About the author

David is an award-winning author with an international reputation as a creative writing tutor and motivational speaker.

His first book, *Can We Talk, Lord?*, was published in 1992 when he was 18. Since then, he has gone on to write for numerous publishers internationally. As well as his many religious books, David is known for walking darker paths with his fiction, his work covering horror and dark fantasy, with the trilogy *The Dead, The Dark,* and *The Damned,* and the standalone novel, *Doomrider,* as well as books for under-confident readers and national reading schemes. David has worked as ghostwriter and researcher for an international best-selling author and also published *Booksurfers,* a four-book series on Kindle written specifically to help children discover classic works such as *Treasure Island* and *A Christmas Carol*. In 2015 he made a guest appearance on a DVD box set to talk about the literary works of Clive Barker.

David lives in Somerset with his two sons, Elijah and Gabriel. When they're not climbing or exploring rivers, they can be found creating the best homemade pizza in the world and chasing each other around his flat with Nerf blasters.

Introduction

Life is stuffed full with moments you never forget. Some you really wish you could, others you happily replay again and again. One for me is this: carrying my first born, Elijah, out of the hospital, in the baby carrier.

It was at that moment that the physical nature of what being a dad meant really hit home. He was no longer just a blip on a heart rate monitor, a swirly picture on a scanner, a strangely fascinating movement on the surface of his mother's tummy. The carrier was heavy. Elijah was heavy. He was a living, breathing, heavy thing, of flesh and bone, and as my arm ached with the walk back to the car that early morning, with every step I knew that I was leaving one life behind and forging a new path into an unknown world.

I will never forget it: the weight of my son in my hand. And it's a weight that grows with every day and sometimes I feel too weak to carry it. At these times, I depend on many things. My friends, my family, the hope in the world I see around me and the God I know who holds me close.

Now, I'm no prize example of just how an awesome father should be. Not in the slightest. I've done things I'm not proud of, I've behaved at times in ways that even now make me shudder. I do not always react as I should, say the things I should, set the example I should. But if I dwell on these moments, then I have no chance of being a father at all. What I can do is learn from them, grow, accept my failures and weaknesses, and do everything in my power to make sure that each and every day I grow stronger, learn from my mistakes and forever hold my children at the centre of what I'm about.

Fatherhood is a wondrous, insane, frustrating, bonkers, frightening, messy, upsetting, terrifying, all-consuming, life-affirming blessing. And it is a blessing I am thankful for each and every day.

As to the prayers and thoughts in this book? Well, if you're expecting the next poet laureate or guru of being a dad to rise, then look elsewhere. That ain't me and that ain't what you'll find here. What you will find – I hope – is honesty and humour. There's no way I could cover all the ups and downs of what every new father experiences and to attempt to would be foolish on my part. Instead, these are snapshots of moments that still stick in my mind, thoughts that at the time were so real and so a part of me that to avoid them would've been impossible. Which, surely, is what God asks of us, right? He wants the real us. The honest us. The broken, bruised, excited, baffled, confused, hopeful, lost, fearful, weeping, laughing 'us'. I'm all of those things. And more. So why should I try to be anything else? I shouldn't. Because if I went down that road, I'd be no father at all.

I love being a dad. I love it more than anything else I've ever done in my life. And I will go on loving it for whatever life I have ahead of me because, through it, I have discovered exactly what unconditional love means. And that? Well, that is everything, I think.

Dave

The News

Oh Lord, it's happened ...
We're pregnant.
Got the call a few minutes ago.
Then a photo of a stick with a blue line on it.
A stick covered in wee.
A stick, I've been told, she'll, 'Never throw away – ever!'

So that's it, then.
A blue line and off we go towards parenthood.

To be honest I don't really know what to feel.
To begin with it was fun, exciting.
Not least because there was more sex.
That's never something to complain about really, is it?
But soon that became some kind of regimented task.
Do it a certain way,
at a certain time of the month,
at a certain time of the day.
Then there was the worry about what if we can't
get pregnant;
Is there something wrong with us?
Is there something wrong with me?
With her?
Is it our diet?
Is it where the bed's placed in the bedroom?
I'm being flippant.
Also, I'm not.
It kind of got like that.
Now though, it's all for real.
The blue line says so.

I think I should feel more than I do.
I should be leaping up and down and cheering.
Running around proud of my manly virility.

I'm not doing any of that.
I'm not really feeling anything.
Except a little bit bad for not feeling anything.
Wasn't really expecting that.

Anyway, Lord, we're pregnant.
Half of us is bouncing around with excitement.
The other half – me – isn't.
We've stepped over that blue line
(the one covered in wee).
And from this point forward,
our lives have changed utterly.
Nothing will be the same again.
Ever.

We're pregnant, Lord.
And now I realise that it's not that I don't
feel anything,
But that I feel everything, all at once,
and I'm speechless.

Amen.

> Now I will tell you of new things
> even before they begin to happen.
> *Isaiah 42:9*

What IS That?

Lord,
I can't see it.
I know I'm supposed to, right?
I've said all the proper things,
oo'ed and ah'd just enough I think,
but really, when you look at it,
all I can see anyway is …
Well, I don't know what I can see.

I know what I wanted to see,
I wanted to see a very obvious little baby,
a mini-me just floating around,
doing what a new baby does.

I didn't see that.
At all.
Instead, I saw some greenish smudge.
It moved a bit, at least I think it did,
at least I said that's what I saw.

Look,
I'm not saying I'm not excited,
it's just that,
well,
it all seems a bit unreal.
Like I'm detatched from what's going on.
Because, really,
I am.

There's nothing growing in me, is there?
All I can do is stand back and watch.
I don't feel, 'the fluttering of butterfly wings' in
my tummy.
Sick with panic at times, yes, but not that.

I'm sounding flippant.
I'm not.
All I want is for this to feel real for both of us.
Properly real.
'Real' real.
Not, 'What on earth is that?' real.

Just a minute, Lord,
there's …
What is that?
A heart?
That's the heart beat?
You're kidding me …

Amen.

You created every part of me;
you put me together in my mother's womb.

Psalm 139:13

How Much?

Lord,
babies are expensive.
I know, because I'm standing at the checkout hoping
to high heaven that this lot clears on my card.
Ours isn't even here yet,
and we've maxed our credit card,
spent our savings,
remortgaged the house,
and sold my parents.

I'm prone to exaggeration, but that's what it feels like.
Every time we go out we spend more money
on stuff I never knew existed
made entirely of colours that are impossible
and designed by people who are undoubtedly from
Planet Baby.

I'll admit, some of it is cute.
What's not to love about a tiny corduroy jacket?
But I can't love it enough to be happy that I just
spent a bazillion pounds on something that'll be
worn once.

Prams, Lord.
This one cost more than my first car.
What's THAT about?
The cot? Well that looks better made than any bed
I've ever slept in.
And so it should be for that price.

Then there's the nappies,
breast pump,
babygros,
baby wipes,
socks (they're properly cute, though, I'll admit that),
baby monitor (that a Special Forces team would
be happy to use to spy on a target it's so
insanely advanced),
wicker basket crib thing,
blankets …

I need another job, Lord,
one that pays three times what I'm on right now.
And then some.
Well, that's how it feels.
Didn't think of any of this at the beginning.
It was all a case of, 'Woohoo! Let's have a baby!
Awesome!'
Now it's more, 'We're having a baby … (massive
silence) …'

Right, best be off.
Plenty more shops to go in I'm sure.
Oh happy day …

Amen.

> Don't worry about anything, but in all your prayers
> ask God for what you need, always
> asking him with a thankful heart.
>
> *Philippians 4:6*

Right, Here We Go …

Lord,
it's happened.
Waters broke.
We're going to have a baby.

I was expecting this to all happen in the middle of the night.
You know, add to the atmosphere and all that.
But it's early afternoon.
And a weekend.
Where's the panic?
Where's the me dashing across town to come to the rescue?

I'm kidding, Lord.
(Ish.)

But this is definitely it.
The baby is on its way.
I'm sure there are things I should be thinking about,
things I should be thanking you for,
but really,
all it boils down to,
is how natural this all feels.
And it does.

There's no panic.
No crushing terror and worry.

Just a sense that this is right;
This is what life is about.
So let's get on with it
and live it.

Time to go say hi to a new person, Lord.

Amen.

> Children are a gift from the Lord;
> they are a real blessing.
> *Psalm 127:3*

He's Blue …

Lord …
My son was blue.
I wasn't expecting that at all.
Out he came, and ignoring the fact that he's
absolutely enormous,
(Aren't babies tiny things? You know, all small and fit
in your hand tiny?)
It was his colour that struck me.
Blue.
Bright BLUE.

Blue.

Not pink at all.

Blue.

Then came a yell,
the sucking in of air,
and the colour changed.
Pink took over.

Life!

I'm lost for words, Lord.
Not something that happens that often.
But this?

A new life which is here because of me and his mum?
Words can't touch it, Lord.
I'm speechless.

But in talking to you,
I know that words aren't always important.
Prayer isn't just me talking.
In fact, the less talking I do,
the more chance I've got of hearing you.

So, Lord,
in this moment when words fail,
hear my silence as a roar of praise,
for this little miracle:
My new son.

Amen.

I will praise you, Lord, with all my heart;
I will tell of all the wonderful things you have done.

Psalm 9:1

The Weight of Life

Lord,
it's 5am
and I'm sitting in my car.
We are all bleary-eyed.
We are all exhausted.
And yet the one thing I'm focusing on
is the pain in my arm.

No, it's not from having my hand crushed
(that did happen though),
but from carrying my son from the hospital
to the car.

Placing him in the baby carrier
he seemed to weigh so little,
and yet,
having carried him,
that weight made itself known.

My arm aches,
and it is a pain I relish.

The weight of life, Lord.
The physical nature of what we have brought into
the world.
It is no longer an idea,
a dream.

It has moved beyond odd alien movements in his mum's stomach,
the joy of decorating a bedroom,
far too many hours spent shopping for yet more stuff he will absolutely, definitely, 'need' …

It is now real.

This boy,
but a few hours old,
is a real thing.
A breathing thing of flesh and bone.
A heartbeat.
A hope for the future.

The weight of life, Lord,
is so much more than mass.
It is a thing built of wonder,
of hope and fear and surprise and joy and yes even more fear.

But ultimately, Lord,
it is something bigger than all of that put together.

He is here.
He is alive.
He is my son.

And I thank you for him.

Amen.

Come to me, all of you who are tired from carrying
heavy loads, and I will give you rest. Take my yoke
and put it on you, and learn from me, because I am
gentle and humble in spirit; and you will find rest.
For the yoke I will give you is easy, and the load
I will put on you is light.

Matthew 11:28-30

First Night

Lord, it's 3am.
I should be in bed,
or at least trying to sleep.
But I'm not.

Instead, I'm downstairs in the lounge,
lights out,
watching a 60s horror film
with the sound turned right down.
And lying in my arms
is my son.

I couldn't be more awake if I tried.
This is the best feeling ever.
Everything about this moment is perfect.
And I don't want to ever forget it.

Upstairs, this new life's mum is fast asleep
(I can hear her snoring)
(not that she snores, obviously …).
The labour was a nightmare.
I was useless.
But we can talk about that some other time.
(Or just forget all about it – my preferred option,
if I'm honest.)
She probably needs to sleep for a year.
Let her.
Or at least let this moment feel like a year.

The warmth of his body is so real.
I know that sounds stupid, because it is real,
but I think you know what I mean.

This is a life, Lord.
In my arms.
A real life we created
because we love each other.

That's an amazing thing:
to create something out of love.
To make something from love.

How can anyone fail to be moved by that?

This moment will last forever, Lord.
I know it.
Yes, it'll be morning soon.
Yes, the sun will break the darkness
and we'll move into a new day,
the start of the rest of this little life.
But this moment, right now?
It's eternal.

Amen.

> I am content and at peace.
> As a child lies quietly in its mother's arms,
> so my heart is quiet within me.
>
> *Psalm 131:2*

Chocolate

If anyone asks me, 'As a parent, what advice would you give to someone expecting their first baby?'
I have this answer!
And the answer is: CHOCOLATE.

Forget everything you've read.
Forget everything you've been told.
Don't worry about spending weeks filling your freezer with ready meals.
Ignore everything anyone's ever told you about how to plan your day,
how to get your baby sleeping,
how to BE THE BEST PARENT EVER.

Instead:
BUY CHOCOLATE.

And lots of it.

Fill the fridge with chocolate.
Have a special tub of the stuff in every room in the house (even the bathroom).
Accept that you will want chocolate with each and every meal.
Have it in the glove box in the car.
Buy it in bulk.

CHOCOLATE.

I'm serious, by the way.
And I know this because I don't even have a sweet tooth.
But that's all changed.
Chocolate is joy.
Chocolate is survival.
Chocolate is my friend.

Which reminds me ... we're running out ...

Amen.

> The joy that the Lord gives you
> will make you strong.
> *Nehemiah 8:10*

Work

I'm at work, Lord.
And I don't want to be.
No change there then, right?
Except there is.
Because it's more important now than ever before
that I work.
Properly.
No messing around.
Take it seriously.
Responsibility, Lord?
That's just hit home big time.

The world's changed, Lord.
We both have jobs.
It's no longer a case of Man Go To Work With
Serious Face While Woman Stay Home Do Baby Stuff.
No.
And I'm glad.

We're a team, Lord.
This is about us working together to bring up this
new child.
And that means both of us earning money,
both of us taking a proper role in being parents.
Which is why I'm feeling a bit rubbish.

I want to be at home.
I want to be with my son and his mum.

I want to be feeding him and joining in
and doing nappies
and bath time
and all the rest of it (which I will be in a few hours,
I know, but you know what I mean, right?).

Instead,
I'm in an office decorated by someone who thought
grey was inspiring.
I'm surrounded by people who are colleagues,
not friends.
I can hear a photocopier being punched,
smell cheap coffee mixed with even cheaper aftershave,
taste the rubbish sandwiches I made for myself in
a rush.

Arguably, I need to pull myself together.
Moping around isn't any good, is it?
A few hours more,
I'll be home,
covered in baby vomit,
and heading into another night of tag-team sleep
'n' feed.

Help me stay focused, Lord.

Amen.

> Trust in God at all times, my people.
> Tell him all your troubles, for he is our refuge.
> *Psalm 62:8*

Who We Are

Lord,
I just got a text from a mate.
He and a few others are out at the pub.
Now I want to be out at the pub.
Is that bad?

It's not that I don't want to be here.
I do.
I love this.
Even when, at three in the morning,
with my toe stubbed yet again in the dark,
and a screaming baby in my arms,
I'm wondering just what the hell we've done,
I still, deep down, love it.
Being a parent.
A dad.
A husband.

But I'd still love a pint right now.
To be in a pub,
having a laugh,
chatting to mates.

I'm being an idiot.
It's not like my life is over, is it?
And it's not like missing the pub is the End of All Things.

I think though,
what I mean is,
that we both need to make sure
we don't get totally swallowed up by all this.
Yes, we're parents,
yes, we have a son (who's clearly the best baby ever),
but we're also people.
Individuals,
and a couple.
We need to remember that.
And make sure we work on it.
Because if we don't?
Exactly, Lord …

Help us remember who we are,
and what we are to each other.

Amen.

> Whatever you do, work at it with all your heart.
> *Colossians 3:23*

Tag Team

Right, Lord,
just a quick prayer before I take my turn.

He's been up for the past two hours,
and we're tag-teaming the night.
It's exhausting.
We're crabby.
And there isn't enough chocolate in the world
to save us from this kind of tiredness.

We're trying our best to be civil,
but it's not easy.
Not with so little sleep for the past few weeks.

I know this is normal.
I know parents have been going through this forever.
Doesn't make it any easier.

Sometimes (actually, a lot of times)
it seems like I can't get anything right.
I can't read him like his mum can,
I don't seem to have the bond she has with him.
I feel useless.
A spare part for a machine that doesn't even
exist here.

This is the tiredness talking, I know that.
We're doing OK.

We make sure each day starts afresh,
no matter the night before.
We apologise (eventually).
We help each other.
And we laugh.

That's the important one there, Lord,
right at the end: laughter.

Without that?

Anyway,
off I go …
I could sleep,
but I'll do that next year.

Amen

> Those who trust in the Lord for help
> will find their strength renewed.
> They will rise on wings like eagles;
> they will run and not get weary;
> they will walk and not grow weak.
>
> *Isaiah 40:31*

Puke Face

Well I should've thought that through really,
shouldn't I, Lord?
Never lift a loaded baby over your head.
Certainly never do it and then shake them a bit.

It's not like there was any warning either.
I got all caught up in the cute-ness of everything,
and got paid for my nonsense
with a face full of baby sick.

This is one of those things which, a few months ago,
would have made me retch.
The thought of such a thing would horrify me.
Now?
It's just another day at the parent-face.
Puke in face?
Done.
Poo in the bath?
Done.
Full nappy kicked up onto one's shoulder?
Yep, done that, too.

Parenthood forces you to view things differently.
It makes you re-evaluate every aspect of who you are,
what you're made of,
what you care about,
and what you don't.

I know what I care about, Lord.
I care about what I have here, right now.
I may smell a little bit of sick,
and I may not be able to get rid of that for the rest of the day,
but disgusting as it may be,
it's a reminder of what all this is worth.

This is family, Lord.
My family.

And that's everything.

Amen

> The Lord will take delight in you,
> and in his love he will give you new life.
> He will sing and be joyful over you.
> *Zephaniah 3:17*

Sex

Lord,
I'd really like to have sex.

It's been a good while now, that's for sure.
No surprise really.
It's pretty impossible to feel in the mood
when the house looks like it's had an
internal haemorrhage,
everything is covered in baby stuff,
your eyes are bloodshot with exhaustion,
your tiredness has made your senses so on edge
that you can hear birds blinking,
and your body just aches from simply being alive.

But I still find myself thinking about it.

Trouble is,
I don't really know how to approach the subject.
Neither of us are in a fit state for a bit of romance,
and a part of me knows it would all be
rather awkward,
what with our minds being on other stuff,
namely the new life we're learning to live with.

It does worry me, though.
Sex is important.
It's a part of what we have.
It's a key part of being married.
Yeah, it creates babies,
but it also creates closeness,

helps bind you together,
reminds you that you're not just two adults
with a child,
but two people
in love
and who fancy each other.

None of that is bad.
No.
All of that is good.

Tonight's probably not the time, Lord.
Tomorrow probably won't be, either.
At some point it will need to be, though.
Because if it isn't?
If it gets forgotten?
Lost under the piles of baby clothes?
Then that's a first step
towards a marriage that isn't.

And I know neither of us
want that to be a step we take.

Help us to remember we love each other, Lord.
Heart, soul and body.

Amen.

> Trust in the Lord with all your heart. Never rely on what you think you know. Remember the Lord in everything you do, and he will show you the right way.
>
> *Proverbs 3:5, 6*

Death

There's something weird, Lord, about looking into
the eyes of a brand new life.
You stare at it,
are amazed by it,
hypnotized by it,
and then suddenly you think:
I'm going to die.

Not right in that moment, obviously.
But there, right in front of you,
is proof that you will die.
After all,
if folk kept on getting born,
and no one died,
we'd pretty soon run out of space.

Mortality is a weird thing.
Life is defined by the fact that it doesn't go on and
on forever.
It ends.
It is finite.
One day, I will not have another day.
One day, that day will be my last day.
One day, I will die.

A part of me panics at this.
I get it quite a lot.
I race through what's left of my life
and before I know it,
I'm 97 and knocking on heaven's door.

Another part of me knows what I believe.
In you.
In what comes after.
In what you've promised.

I'm not being morbid (at least I hope I'm not).
Death is a part of life.
In fact the biggest cause of death
is being alive.
Being born.

So here I am,
staring at this new life.
It's gurgling at me now,
head wobbling all over the place.

I could worry about death.
I could sit here and get all scared about when that moment comes
and I take my last breath.

Or I could sit here
and gaze in wonder at the creation in my hands
and count myself blessed to be alive at all.

I think I know which one I'm going to go with.

Amen.

> Everything that happens in this world
> happens at the time God chooses.
> He sets the time for birth and the time for death.
>
> *Ecclesiastes 3:1, 2*

Night Drive

Well, once again I'm doing something I said I
wouldn't do:
Taking my newborn son
for a drive in the car
in the middle of the night
to get him to sleep.

I knew other parents did this.
Fools, I thought.
Fancy letting the baby rule their lives!
Pah!
I'd never do something so idiotic.
Absolutely never ever.

Wrong.
So very, very wrong.
Because we need to sleep.
And for us to sleep
we need him to sleep.
Desperately.

It's been five nights on the trot now.
No one seems to have had more than two hours in
any one stretch.
Our skin is grey with weariness.
Our eyes have sunk into the back of our skulls.
We're snappy,

grumpy,
angry,
hungry.
Just plain knackered, Lord.
Which means I probably shouldn't be driving ...

But at least he's asleep, Lord.
And at least I know his mum is, too,
and neither will she be woken by the faintest
of sounds.
Like, for example,
the blink of an eye ...

Lord,
there's no preparation for this, is there?
None at all.
Yes, there are way too many books on the subject,
all written by experts in their field,
all with thousands of converts,
and all saying the exact opposite of every
other expert.
Yet when it comes down to it,
the only way to learn to be a parent
is to just get on with it
and hope that you're doing it OK.

Mistakes happen.
Bad days come round far too often.
But there are glimmers of hope.
Like now,
as I look in my mirror,

and see behind me,
a peaceful face
barely a few weeks' old.

He's asleep, Lord.
Beautifully.

Amen.

> The Lord is my shepherd;
> I have everything I need.
> He lets me rest in fields of green grass
> and leads me to quiet pools of fresh water.
> He gives me new strength.
> *Psalm 23:1-3*

HELP!
I'm a New Dad!

I'm No Good at This

Lord,
I can't do this.
I'm just no good at being a parent.

Thankfully, my son seems OK.
But then his mum has this paranormal superpower
when it comes him.
She can read his mind
when in another room.
She can understand what he needs
through solid concrete.

Me?
Well yes, me …

What can I do?
Sometimes, it seems like it would be easier
to say the things I can't.

Such as:
feed him properly;
know when he should be awake/asleep;
dress him in clothes that match;
dress him in clothes appropriate for the 15 types of
weather we experience each and every day;
clean all the things he might come into contact
with …

Then there's other stuff I really can't even
think about,
like what school he should go to,
what university.

I kid you not, Lord: university!
I mean, he's only a few months' old
and these are the very things his mum is
concerned about!
And then I get it in the neck
because frankly I'm more concerned about getting
through the next week without us killing each other
than what degree this newborn will do.
And I'd best not dare suggest he might not go to
university either …

I'm being flippant.
And, if I might say so,
a bit pathetic.

I understand the worry.
Deep down, these concerns are mine, too.
And with each of them
my worry is that I will never do a good enough job
as a dad
to ensure that my son
makes the best decisions
for himself.

I fear that my guidance will be off,

my example bad,
that one day he'll look at me and be,
well,
disappointed.

I'm just me, Lord.
I'm no superhero.
But then again,
neither is my own father,
and all things considered,
he's done a pretty decent job.

I'm rambling.
I do that a lot at the moment.
Blame it on the lack of sleep.

I can do this, Lord.
I can be a dad.
I have to be.
I am.

Amen.

> I said, 'I am falling';
> but your constant love, O Lord, held me up.
> *Psalm 94:18*

HELP!
I'm a New Dad!

Date Night

Right, Lord,
just a quick word before I move away from this mirror
and head downstairs.

Somehow,
we've managed to persuade someone
to babysit.
And by someone
I mean my mother-in-law
who from this point forward
I shall refer to as a saint.

We've left a list of everything that needs to be done,
about a thousand contact numbers,
full details of where we'll be – including a map –
and we're about to head off out
together.

Just us.
On a date.

Can't say I'm impressed with how I look.
Bags under the eyes.
More grey hair, I'm sure.
And I certainly don't fill this shirt out in the right places any more.

Crikey ... I'm hideous ...
Best not to dwell ...

This is important for us.
It's going to be weird being out, alone,
no baby.

I'm nervous.
Actually, I'm pretty terrified.
What if we don't like each other?
What if all we can talk about is the baby?
What if we don't fancy each other?
What if ...

What if ...

What if,
despite all my worries,
tonight is OK?
What if we enjoy being together?
What if we laugh and joke,
talk about our new son,
but also about other stuff,
perhaps plan another night out?

Right,
best get my game face on.
Time to impress.
And I want to, Lord.
I want her to look at me when I appear downstairs
and think, 'Hey, he's not too bad on the eye ...'

I want her to love me.
And I want to love her.

After all,
it's why we had a baby in the first place, isn't it?
Love?

Amen.

Fill your minds with those things that are good and
that deserve praise: things that are
true, noble, right, pure, lovely, and honourable.
Philippians 4:8

HELP!
I'm a New Dad!

Baby Food

It's green, Lord.
Green.
Can't think of any other way to describe it.
GREEN.

And now here I am trying to spoon the stuff into a
tiny mouth.
A mouth which moves in the manner
of a goldfish's.

I can't remember what went into this,
but I've no doubt it's 100% organic
(as is everything he eats,
because being responsible parents
means everything has to be organic, apparently,
even his socks).

Our freezer is rammed
with little blocks of frozen green.
I open the door
and feel like I'm on the set of a sci-fi movie,
like I've stumbled on some secret lab.
And in the frozen depths,
behind the far-too-old fish fingers,
is something that will bring humanity to its knees …

Does he like it?
Not sure.
What do you think?
I'm not convinced any of it has actually gone into his mouth yet.
There's a fair amount of it on his forehead
(no idea how it got there)
and – yep – there's some behind his ears and,
even more amazingly,
on the back of his neck.

I seem to be wearing a lot of it as well, Lord.
It's everywhere.
The Green is taking over!
Help!

This is brilliant, Lord.
I'm feeding a tiny new human!
Me!
Feeding my son!
With green stuff!

Now he's got the spoon
and he's sticking it in his ear.
Nope – he's throwing it on the floor.
Has ... he has thrown it on the floor.

Lord,
I'm enjoying this.
I might even start thinking soon that I'm getting the hang of it.

This whole being-a-dad thing?
I can do it.

I had a fear that my clumsiness
would result in untold damage,
that I'd lose the baby behind the sofa,
or accidentally twang him into a tree,
or see him roll off down a hill in his pram.

None of this has happened.
We're all still here!
And here I am,
feeding him.

Thank you, Lord.

Thank you for all of this.
Even the green slime now in my eye …

Amen.

> Praise the Lord, my soul!
> I will praise him as long as I live;
> I will sing to my God all my life.
>
> *Psalm 146:1, 2*

HELP!
I'm a New Dad!

The Timetable

Lord,
I have an urge to burn every diary ever printed.
I want to take every daily plan,
every spreadsheet,
every timetable ever created,
pile them all up,
and set fire to them.

I now exist in a world
where my every moment
seems to be cut up into 10 and 15-minute segments.
Right down to when I wake up,
have breakfast,
go for a walk …

The thing is,
I kind of support it.
Sometimes.
Other times?
Other times I want us to relax a bit,
but we can't.
We just keep on following this plan
and it's getting on my nerves.

Everything is centred on what we do with the baby.
Everything.
That's all that seems to matter.
And I'm as guilty as anyone.

So any blame I'm throwing
comes back at me as much as going anywhere else.
Makes me want to scream though.

I was never one for a regimented life.
I need a bit of give in any plan.
The tighter a plan gets,
the more I want to break out of it.

OK ... deep breaths ...
This isn't just about me.
It's about all of us.
Plans work.
Plans make sense.
If we didn't have a plan
this place would be total chaos
rather than only slightly chaotic.

We just need to work together, Lord.
Listen to each other,
support each other,
allow a little give and take,
and fall back on that love that brought us together
in the first place.

Amen.

> We may make our plans, but God has the last word ...
> Ask the Lord to bless your plans, and you will
> be successful in carrying them out.
>
> *Proverbs 16:1, 3*

Reading

Lord,
I'm sitting here,
my baby son in my lap,
and we're reading a book together.

Okay, so perhaps reading isn't quite the right term,
but there's a book involved,
and we're looking at it!

This is awesome!
I'm reading a book with my son!

Nothing gets better than this.
Just me and him,
flicking through some pages,
pointing at a dinosaur
(because, as we all know, all babies love
dinosaurs, right?)

The story's pretty simple.
On each page
we discover it isn't actually our dinosaur we're looking at
because it's too fluffy/squashy/smooth/bouncy/
bobbly …

What I'm loving is seeing those little hands trying
to explore.
I'm helping,
moving the book closer,
holding his hands in mine,
showing him what's on each page.
And we're talking, too.
Or something like talking.
I'm sure he understands me,
and I think I know what the sounds he makes mean.
Not that it matters.
This moment is golden, regardless.

It's the times like this, Lord,
that make me realise what it's all about.
The tiredness,
the confusion,
the worry,
they all get in the way,
then something like this burns all of that to a crisp,
and I'm left in bewildered awe
at this first-hand experience
of love's creation.

Thank you.

Amen.

Praise the Lord!
With all my heart I will thank the Lord.

Psalm 111:1

What About Me?

Lord,
this sounds so pathetic,
and I'm ashamed to admit it, really,
but …
I'm jealous.
Of my son.

Admitting it makes it seem even worse.
How can I be feeling like this?
Makes no sense!
He's just a few months' old.
He's brand spanking new to the world.
And I'm jealous?
What is wrong with me?

This is embarrassing, Lord.
I've told no one about this, clearly.
It's not exactly something you can openly admit.
And it's absolutely something I don't want to discuss out loud.

So it's just me and you on this.
OK?
Good.

This isn't a feeling or an emotion I was expecting, Lord.
Not in the slightest.

I knew I would be tired,
stressed,
worried,
not jealous though.

I've been back at my job for a while now
and I think that's part of it.
I miss being at home.
I miss being with my son.
Which means I'm jealous of my wife, as well!
Oh, for goodness sake …

I am, though, Lord. I really I am.
I want to be at home,
looking after him,
playing with him,
singing stupid gurgly nonsense songs to him
while he splashes in the bath.

I knew my wife's time would be totally taken up
by being a mother.
That's fine.
That's good.
The way it should be.
But sometimes I think,
not so much, 'What about me?',
but
'What about us?'
I'm not saying we used to have this crazy wild
social life.
But we did go out.

And we did do stuff together.
Now though it's just baby this
and baby that
and who would look after him
and maybe next month …

Saturdays still seem to comprise of yet another trip
to Baby Land
where we spend even more money
on loads more baby stuff.
Then back home (by a specific time or the lad will
NEVER SLEEP AGAIN)
to more baby stuff and an evening/night of
tag-teaming.

Sundays are a repeat of Saturdays.
Then the week starts up again and I'm sitting at
my desk.

Lord,
I don't think I ever really thought that much
about the difference all this would make
to the time we have to be just 'us',
as individuals.
As a couple.
I don't regret it – the opposite, in fact.
I love being a dad.
But I need to get back to being a husband, too.

Maybe that's what this is.
I need to focus on her a bit more,

make her feel special,
loved,
not just as a mum,
but as my wife.

Got it, Lord.

Amen.

> Look out for one another's interests,
> not just for your own.
> *Philippians 2:4*

What If I'm Not a Good Dad?

I've got The Fear, Lord …
My stomach's all twisted up,
I can't focus,
my mind's doing a whirlpool with its thoughts.
Why?
Simple:
I'm worried I'm not a good dad.

Early days, I know,
but I still worry.
Can't help it.

I'm worried I won't set a good example,
that who I am
is not what this new life should see,
look up to.
I'm nothing special by any measure.
I make mistakes,
foul things up,
bad decisions seem to be a part of my every day.
Is this really what I want my boy to see?

I need to be a strong father, Lord.
Perfect.
I need to be the kind of person
my son looks up to
because that person
is pretty awesome at everything.

Me?
I'm not awesome at anything.
I'm just a plain, normal, human being.
I'm riddled with contradictions,
errors,
problems,
worries.

The thing is though,
if I even attempt at being someone who's all perfect,
then I'm not being honest,
truthful.
And those two things
are key to being a dad.

It's not about being perfect,
because that word comes with a lot of baggage.
And anyway, we all have different views of what
it means.
Perhaps, Lord,
my role as a dad
is to just be me.
To love my son with all that I am.
To be honest enough to share my life with him,
warts and all.
Mistakes are a part of what life is,
and we learn from them.
I'm not superman.
I'm just me.

But perhaps being 'Just Me'
is exactly what being a dad is all about.
No lies.
Nothing hidden.
Unconditional love.

Amen.

> **We love because God first loved us.**
> *1 John 4:19*

HELP!
I'm a New Dad!

Nappies

Lord,
I can't really speak
because I'm gagging
at what lies before me
and has just been kicked all over the wall.

I knew nappies would be bad,
but you get used to it pretty sharpish.
Having a baby means no real time to get squeamish
about stuff like this.
Some though,
well,
they're epic.
Like this one.

I need an NBC suit, Lord.
Well, I did,
but now it's pretty pointless,
as my eyes are watering,
and I've just realised it's not just gone all over
the wall
but all over me, too.
Still, he seems happy, doesn't he?

Right,
best get on with cleaning him up.
No real reason to this prayer, Lord;
Just figured I'd share a moment with you.

A small part of fatherhood,
which is just as important as any other part.
Because I'm involved with my child,
I'm looking after him,
and somehow I'm smiling,
even through the poop.

Amen.

> Love is patient and kind ... Love never gives up;
> and its faith, hope, and patience never fail.
> *I Corinthians 13:4, 7*

Natural Bond

Lord,
since the birth,
I've been watching my son and his mum
and noticed something.
There's a bond there, Lord.
Something almost supernatural.
Maybe it is supernatural.
It goes beyond words,
beyond actions,
it just 'is'.

It's a beautiful thing, Lord.
An invisible force seems to bind them.
It makes sense that such a thing would exist.
You don't walk around with a new human growing inside you
and not have some connection to them, right?

Sometimes,
it's as though they both have a sixth sense.
They'll know when the other is in the next room.
Mum will know if something is wrong with her son
even before he does.
Or that's the way it seems.
It's an amazing thing, Lord.
Otherworldly.

I think I have a sort of a bond, Lord.
But it doesn't seem quite so natural.
I want it to be.

I really want to sense all the things my son's mum is able to,
but it doesn't seem to be quite the same.
Again, why should it?
I didn't carry him.
I didn't have him grow in me.
(It's something that, once witnessed, humbles you for eternity I think.)
Mind, I did poke him a few times when he was at a weird angle!
A foot here,
a bottom there,
wriggling around in an alien fashion.

Your creation is a breathtaking thing, Lord.
The science can explain it,
down to the smallest molecule,
but that really only adds to the wonder.
Add in the bond between mother and son?
I am ... speechless.

Thank you, Lord,
for all of this.
For them.

Amen.

You will be like a child that is nursed by its mother,
carried in her arms, and treated with love.
I will comfort you ... as a mother comforts her child.

Isaiah 66:12, 13

Career Vs Dad

Lord,
for years it was pretty much all about me.
Do college,
get a job,
off we go.
Getting married changed 'me' to 'us'
but didn't really alter the importance of the job side
of things.
It was a way to security,
provided a house,
a bit of extra cash.
Now though, it feels very different.

What I'm saying, Lord,
is that it's pretty hard to care about anything else now
other than my family.
Career, and all that's wrapped up in that word,
seems so pointless.
I know it's not,
I know I need a job,
even more so now than ever,
but it's harder than ever
and all because of that little human being
we decided to bring into this world.

Sitting at my desk,
my mind wanders more.
I want to be home,

I want to be with my wife,
my son.
I want to be right there,
in it.

I have to be here, though, Lord.
I know it.
If I'm not here,
then we have no roof over our heads,
no food.
Pretty important stuff, really.

And it'll be worse for his mum, too,
when she heads back,
as she will.
No choice really.
And the wrench will be tough on them both.

So my job, Lord,
is to crack on, right?
Head down, get the job done,
and support them both.
I can't be there as much as I want to be,
but when I am, I know that the times I'm away
I'm not neglecting,
but the opposite.
I'm providing.
Or trying to.

We both are, Lord.
Each day,

every minute of every hour,
providing for our son.
Working things through together.
The good times,
the tough.

All of it for him.
And through it all,
growing closer,
growing stronger.

Amen.

The Lord says, 'When Israel was a child I loved him
and called him out of Egypt as my son …
I was the one who taught Israel to walk.
I took my people up in my arms …
I drew them to me with affection and love.
I picked them up and held them to my cheek;
I bent down to them and fed them.'

Hosea 11:1, 3, 4

HELP!
I'm a New Dad!

Separate Beds

Lord,
I know why I'm here,
in the spare room.
And it's not because I've been kicked out
like a stinking dog.
The fact is
I'm here
because we both need some sleep,
particularly my boy's mum.
She's exhausted,
and having me lying next to her,
taking up all the space in the bed?
Well, that's not very helpful, is it?

The thing is,
(and I can say this to you, but keep it to
yourself, OK?)
this isn't the first time,
and I doubt it will be the last.
Some weeks this has actually become all too common.
And I don't like it.

I'm not actually talking about sex here, Lord.
I'm really not.
I'm talking about marriage.
Being together.
Sharing.

And the bed is a part of that.
Sleeping in a separate room isn't what either of us
signed up for.
Why would anyone?

Sometimes,
a separate bed feels pretty awesome!
It's a mix of feeling like a kid again,
and that freedom to just stretch out and zzzzzz …
But really,
deep down,
it feels wrong.

At the moment, Lord,
this is a temporary thing.
It's something done to help out,
to give a bit of space,
allow recovery.
What we both need to be aware of, though, Lord,
is that it could become a habit.
The norm.
And that would be bad.

Separate beds is not the norm
in the same way that not holding hands
is not the norm;
in the same way that not smiling at each other,
not hugging,
not touching,
is not the norm.

We got married, Lord,
because we wanted to be together,
forever.
That's what it was
and is
about.
Together isn't separate rooms, Lord.

So,
as I lay me down to sleep,
help us both remember, Lord,
the other person on the other side of the wall,
and that even though this rest will do us both good,
we belong together,
side by side.

Amen.

> That is why a man leaves his father
> and mother and is united with his wife,
> and they become one.
> *Genesis 2:24*

Laugh

Lord,
I think I have stumbled upon a sound
which would wake me from a coma:
My baby's laugh!

What a sound!

So much joy,
so much happiness,
so much innocence,
all wrapped up in a giggle
that gives me goosebumps.

I could listen to it for hours, Lord.
It's a sound I never tire of.
Never will, either.

Thank you.

Amen.

> Sing a new song to the Lord!
> Sing to the Lord, all the world!
> Sing to the Lord, and praise him.
> *Psalm 96:1, 2*

First Words

Lord,
he said a word!
A proper, actual, real word.
Not a burp
or a garbled google
or a string of sounds
but a word.

And the word?
Prepare yourself …

BANDSTAND!

I kid you not.
Bandstand!
I mean, why?
What on earth does that have to do with anything
at all, ever?
Not dad.
Not mum.
Not dog or cat or pig (words all children's
programmes and books seem to be convinced are
the words all babies need to know above all others)
or food or drink,
but bandstand.

The local park has a bandstand.
It's like any normal bandstand.
Hardly something to commit to memory.
Not exactly life-changing.
And yet now,
for the rest of my life,
it will be.

We're funny, us humans,
aren't we, Lord?
The weirdest things become important to us.
Trinkets we carry around.
Pebbles and shells from a long-ago beach.
A postcard pinned to a fridge.
And now the word 'bandstand'.

Thank you, Lord,
for the small things.

Amen.

> Praise him, kings and all peoples,
> princes and all other rulers;
> young women and young men,
> old people and children too.
> Let them all praise the name of the Lord!
> *Psalm 148:11-13*

Just the Beginning …

Right, Lord,
I'm sitting down.
Just need a moment, OK?
Reason?
Simple: I've just been poleaxed by the enormity of all this.

I'm a parent, Lord.
I have a child.
A human being I brought into this world.
That's no small thing, is it?
The responsibility of it all
just crashed into me
with all the tact of a runaway truck
and I feel a little dazed.

There's so much to think about now.
So much to worry about.
And I don't do worry very well.
It infects everything else.
I forget things.
I get muddled.
I get stressed.

What have I done, Lord?
What have WE done?

I don't think we're ready.
Not for this.
Not for all that it means
and will require.

Being a parent is a lifetime.
That's what it is.
Yes, I'm me still,
but I'm so much more now,
or at least I have to be.
No choice.
Not sure I'm up to it, Lord …

And yet …
And yet I know that I am.
Not because I think I've got this all under control
(far from it)
but because I want this.
I want this more than anything.
I want to be the best dad that I can be
to this new life.
I want to help my child grow,
to learn,
to become the best possible human being he can be.
I want to help him when things are tough,
guide him,
laugh and cry with him,
be there for him
no matter what.

I'm a dad, Lord.
It's my job.
My life.
My everything.

Amen.

> Teach children how they should live,
> and they will remember it all their life.
> *Proverbs 22:6*

HELP!
I'm a New Dad!

An Amazing Mum

Lord,
I want to say thank you
on behalf of my son
for the mum he has in his life.

She's amazing, Lord.
Properly amazing.
Breathtakingly so, if I'm honest.

The pregnancy was tough,
with constant sickness,
backache,
and all the rest that comes along with those
nine months.
As for the birth?
Well, we won't talk of that ever again, if it's all the same with you.
And that in itself says enough, right?
But through all that, there was always the excitement about being a mum.
That never wavered,
only grew stronger.

Now, Lord,
with our son here with us,
I see the woman I met so long ago
as so much more than I could have ever believed.

She is strong, Lord.
Caring.
Loving.
She's so natural at this,
was born for it.
Without her
we wouldn't be making half as good a job of
being parents
as we are.
Ignoring the fact she's read almost every book on the subject,
she just seems to know what to do
and how to do it.
I'm humbled by her, Lord.
Constantly so.

Sometimes I worry
that I can't actually match up
to everything that she now is.
She's become so much more than what she was,
but what if I haven't?
What if she sees me as less now?

I'm sounding paranoid.
But when faced with someone doing something so well?
It's hard not to see that as a blazing light on all the stuff
I get wrong.

But you know what?
None of that matters.
Because we're in this together.
All three of us.
And even in the worst moments,
when sleep is a distant memory,
when nerves are frayed,
when we're hanging by a thread,
I count myself as the luckiest man alive
to have met the woman that I did,
who became the mother of my child.

Thank you, Lord,
for her.

Amen.

> As for my family and me, we will serve the Lord.
> *Joshua 24:15*

Also available in the series

HELP! I'm a New Mum!
1501554

Order from
www.kevinmayhew.com